Hilltop Rescue

Contents

Written by Sarah Loader

Hilltop rescue teams help those who get stuck while out hiking.

They could be lost or hurt.

Lost on the hilltop

Hikers could get lost on a hilltop.

If the rescue team can get through
by phone, they can tell them where
to go.

If the rescue team thought
a person was hurt, they would
have a bigger job.

They might have to carry the person down the hill or pull them on a bed with wheels.

Rescue dogs

Dogs help with rescues at night and if it is hard to see.

Dogs can be used to find tracks that lead to where a person is.

Water on the hilltop

Sometimes there are lakes at the top of hills. Rivers can run through the hilltops too.

Rescue teams may have to pull a
person out of the water.

They help them to get dry and give
them new things to put on.

Going out on the hills is fun,
but have a safe attitude.

Top tips!

- You should not go out in fog or snow.
- You should not push a person
  on the hilltop.

- You should stay on the track.
- You should have a good coat. You do not want to get wet through!

Remember that it is not safe to hike alone. If you wish to go out on the hilltops, ask someone to go with you!